FlexCCarry℠ Solutions
A Positive Guide for Off-Body Carry

What Works in Your Life, for Your Life

Written by
Vicki Farnam

With Collaboration From
Gloria Krauklis, Wendi Lankister,
Marty Rudd, Gary Rudd, and S. Cook

FlexCCarry℠ Solutions: A Positive Guide for Off-Body Carry
By Vicki Farnam

Copyright © 2024 by Vicki Farnam.
First Edition: September 2024
Fourth printing with minor updates: January 2025
Published by Mark Kraemer, Launch Pad Publications LLC

For more information or to book an event, visit
http://www.flexccarry.com

ISBN - 979-8-9916724-0-5 (paperback)
ISBN - 979-8-9916724-1-2 (ebook)

Warning and Disclaimer

Dedications

To John, who has never said to me, "You can't do that."

-Vicki Farnam

To the "Mama Bears" who take personal responsibility
for defending themselves and the littles in their care.

-Wendi Lankister

I dedicate this guide to my husband Ron for his forever support.

-Gloria Krauklis

My contributions are only possible with the support of my loving husband, Gary,
our friends and family who share our passion, and our off-body carry students
who seek training to be their best.

-Marty Rudd

This guide is dedicated to everyone who has carried off-body but was afraid to
admit it. You are the inspiration for this guide, which establishes FlexCCarry℠
as the gold standard.

-Gary Rudd

For the warriors. Whether you have discovered the warrior within or not,
if you are reading this, you are on the path forward.

-S Cook

About the Author

Vicki Farnam has been a firearms trainer for many years. Long ago, she acquired her first handbag with a dedicated pocket for concealed carry! Since then, she has traveled the country teaching classes alongside her husband, John Farnam, DTI, LLC. Along the way, she developed her own specialty of teaching male instructors in the particulars of training women. She has taught that class at numerous law enforcement agencies, academies, and conferences, both local and federal, and she has taught for the US Marine Corps. She is the author of two previous books on teaching firearms to women. In 2019, Vicki began teaching off-body concealed carry, now known as FlexCCarry℠.

Collaborators

This combined project (the Instructor's Certification Course and this Guide) resulted from the dedication of those who have assisted the author through hours of instructional challenges with students on the range in heat, snow, wind, and rain, as well as late-night hours of discussions. Wendi Lankister, Gloria Krauklis, Marty Rudd, Gary Rudd, and S Cook have been invaluable in establishing the topic of off-body carry, now referred to by us as FlexCCarry℠, as a functional and justifiable addition to the body of knowledge of defensive firearms skills.

Acknowledgments

I would like to acknowledge the individuals and organizations that have supported this journey to develop FlexCCarry℠ Solutions :

- Claudia Chisholm, GTM
- Jennifer Wilhelm, GTM
- Rhonda Sega Moore, GTM
- Emanuel Kapelsohn, Attorney
- Carol Craighead, Crossbreed Holsters
- Stacy Bright, Crossbreed Holsters
- Julie Willis, Zendira
- Karen Butler, Shoot Like A Girl
- Christa Clayton Forrester, Shoot Like A Girl
- Pete Lucarelli
- Mayan, UUB
- Cindy Deck Wahlig, UUB
- Robyn Sandoval, A Girl and A Gun
- Sandra Woodruff, A Girl and A Gun
- Marti Stonecipher, Armed Women of America
- Claude Werner
- Martin Hoffert
- Massad Ayoob
- Dana Liesengang
- Heath Gunz, Spoken Outdoors
- Shelley Hill, The Complete Combatant
- James Nowak, Undersheriff
- Mike Barham, Galco Leather
- Brad Tallis, Photographer
- Mark Kraemer
- Travis Ferguson, Cameleon Bags
- Suzanne Freehauf
- All Instructors who have graciously hosted or attended the DTI OBCC Instructor Course
- Sarah Hauptman, PHLstr
- Taalyr Claridge, Church and State Designs
- Coronado Leather
- UC Leather
- Travelon
- Great Guns Sporting, LLC

Contents

Preface

DTI, LLC, began to offer a certification course for Off-Body Concealed Carry Instructors (OBCC) in the fall of 2019 at the request of a major manufacturer who was looking for a curriculum to train instructors who would, in turn, train customers to use their products.

Claudia Chisholm has dedicated her company, GTM Originals (GTM), to manufacturing a wide variety of concealed carry handbags, tote bags, sling bags, and briefcases for women and men to provide a means to carry concealed handguns for self-defense. Claudia insisted that competently trained instructors be available to offer the best education to women and men who wish to purchase a GTM handbag. However, she was not stuck on having only GTM products represented or GTM customers in classes. The first class, conducted in Colorado, consisted of women associated with GTM, but other independent instructors also attended. That first class was a huge success!

Since 2019, we have held classes nationwide and in all weather conditions, ranging from blazing hot, humid, and dusty to cold, snowy, mid-teens temperatures. Dedicated groups of men and women have taken the risk of learning something new to share with students. The weather conditions and locations have tested both the instructors and the products. Which materials hold up best in what kind of weather? During these harsh conditions, we realized that we could reach a handgun faster if it was in a Daily Go Bag hanging on the outside of layers of cold-weather gear instead of in a waistband holster. What a comforting realization!

We also discovered that products from other companies could be paired with GTM. Crossbreed Modular Holsters are ideal. Their VELCRO™ backing adheres to the VELCRO™ in the dedicated pocket of GTM and other brands and provides a handgun-specific Kydex holster to secure any handgun. Carol Craighead, CEO, and Stacy Bright, Social Media Manager at Crossbreed, have supported the Flex-CCarry℠ Instructor Certification classes and enthusiastically provide holsters for most current brands or models of handguns.

Women-owned companies, such as UUB and Zendira, are wonderful supporters. Mayan and Cindy offer the UUB non-purse, and Zendira offers functional, beautiful products for men and women. Julie Willis of Zendira has attended the Instructor class, as well as Fundamentals of Defensive Shooting classes, to test her products and continue her learning

Karen Butler and Christa Forrester of Shoot Like a Girl have sought education for their staff of trainers so they can pass on powerful information on FlexCCarry^{SM} Solutions to their guests. And thanks to them for pushing the concept of FlexCCarry^{SM} Solutions and encouraging progress in the form of this guide.

These companies and these women are the future of this industry. We applaud them for their involvement and their determination that fewer women become victims of criminal violence because they have a fighting chance. We are grateful to all of them for the very existence of FlexCCarry^{SM} Solutions and this guide.

Search the pages of this guide. Find what works for you. Use it daily, and know that you are not alone! Make informed decisions regarding the options and equipment you will need to use. Be courageous in deciding your future as an armed citizen, "*in* your life, *for* your life"!

Introduction

This guide is about the mechanics of your FlexCCarry℠ Daily Go Bag (DGB) choice and the way it works *in* your life, *for* your life. "FlexCCarry℠ Solutions" is a more accurate description of handbags, sling bags, backpacks, tote bags, waist packs, and briefcases with dedicated pockets to hold your handgun than the term "off-body carry."

"Off-body carry" has long been commonly misrepresented by the image of a handgun simply thrown into a purse full of the usual stuff. Whether or not that image is always correct, it is still the prevailing image. It has led to the entire concept of off-body carry being thoroughly vilified by many defensive handgun skills instructors. While that image is sometimes correct, it is not the method that well-trained and knowledgeable women and men use for carrying when a traditional waistband belt with an attached holster is not an option.

The traditional purse usually has some kind of strap attached to either hang off a shoulder, to reach across and around the body, or to hold in the hand.

But wait! How can a technique be identified as "off-body" carry when a strap is attached to the bag, which is then attached to you? Isn't a belt a type of strap attached to you, too? And why is a belt the only type of strap most knowledgeable instructors allow?

What is most important? *Where* a handgun is carried for self-defense, or *if* a handgun is carried for self-defense? If a handgun is carried for self-defense, can it only be carried on a waistband belt with a holster attached to it? Or, can it also be carried in a dedicated pocket in a FlexCCarry℠ Daily Go Bag with a strap attached to the upper body, above the belt?

Wardrobe styles, work requirements and environments, physical challenges, and medical issues are just a few reasons someone may choose or be compelled to choose something other than a waistband belt holster. Who are we firearms instructors who may not have those issues to dictate and demand that someone else use traditional carry to defend themselves or suffer the slings and arrows of ridicule?

IMPORTANT!

This Guide does not replace training specifically for you with your handgun of choice for concealed carry purposes. Seek training on that topic first! This book is about an isolated topic within the field of defensive handgun skills of how to choose, set up, draw from and re-holster to a FlexCCarry℠ Methods Daily Go Bag of your choice.

Before you put your concealed carry handgun in a FlexCCarry℠ DGB:

- **Seek Training from a reputable trainer for you and your personal defensive handgun.**

- **Learn the universal Safety Rules.**

- Learn how your personal handgun functions.

- Practice correct trigger finger placement on the frame (Register Position) while handling your handgun.

- Understand the importance of muzzle control and awareness.

- When learning this process, it is essential to practice first with a blue gun, then with an empty handgun with an empty magazine in the magazine well, and finally with a loaded handgun.

- Once you are ready to practice with a loaded handgun, practice only on a live fire range.

Chapter 1

Misconceptions and Advantages of FlexCCarry℠

As long as there have been small pistols, even dating back to the eighteenth century, women have put them in their drawstring pouch, known as a reticule, for self-protection. Men could put them in their pockets or tuck them in their waistbands, while women's attire did not allow for such convenience. This is where the off-body controversy started.

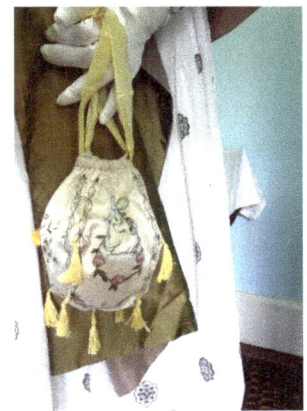

In the modern defensive shooting world, off-body carry is often vilified as a poor choice. The vision of a woman's purse has expanded from a small drawstring pouch to a bag capable of holding everything, including the kitchen sink! Although it may be better to leave the kitchen sink at home so you have room for your handgun!

A Reticule from the 18th Century

Come with us, and we will show you how FlexCCarry℠ Solutions and a Daily Go Bag (DGB) can work *in* your life, *for* your life. Let's look at common misconceptions and advantages.

Misconceptions

Throwing a handgun in a bag with lots of other stuff in it is dangerous because any number of things (keys, lipstick, pen) could get inside the trigger guard and apply unwanted pressure to the trigger, and the handgun could go off. And that's true. The FlexCCarry℠ Solution is a Daily Go Bag deliberately manufactured with a dedicated pocket to hold the handgun in a secured holster that completely covers the trigger. Multiple manufacturers produce bags that meet these criteria. They are not difficult to find.

Young girl with her handbag

One might assume that you will forget your bag or leave it unattended. Most women know where their purse is at all times. Little girls are taught to keep track of their "valuables" when they are given their first handbag. People make mistakes all the time. We can and must commit to doing better and be vigilant about the responsibility we take regardless of how we carry a handgun. Remembering your DGB is no different than remembering not to leave your handgun that you removed from a traditional holster while in a restroom.

One may also assume that someone will come along and try to take the bag away from you forcefully. This happens daily whether there is a handgun in the bag or not. We must not ignore the fact that handguns have also been stolen out of waistband holsters attached to a belt. The risk of not being able to defend your life with your handgun far outweighs the risk of your purse (bag) being stolen.

Yet another assumption is that drawing from a bag is slower than drawing from a waistband holster attached to a belt. In self-defense, speed is relative. The decision to draw is based on circumstances, not a timer. Efficiency is important. Our efficiency is based on our capabilities. Presenting our defensive handgun from a bag may represent a "surprise" and thus an advantage.

You may have seen internet videos demonstrating shooting from inside of a bag. This is a poor idea because it doesn't work. It doesn't work because you don't know where the bullet is going to go. It could hit a zipper, a seam, or other objects in the bag which would deflect its trajectory. Also, the handgun will likely malfunction after the first shot, and you've thus lost your ability to defend yourself further. **Don't let the threat get that close!**

Advantages

FlexCCarry℠ offers numerous advantages that are not available with traditional on-body carry methods. Let's review them!

Women have resisted the request of men in their lives to carry a handgun because they didn't want to change their wardrobe. The FlexCCarry℠ solution allows her the freedom to dress in her own style. She does not have to adjust her wardrobe to accommodate a handgun attached to a particular place on her body. Think of the carry bag as a "Daily Go

Waistband holster

Bag" (DGB). Instead of changing her wardrobe, she can pick a bag that complements her style.

No matter what you are wearing—a dress, a lightweight vest, or your wool sweater, down vest, and heaviest down jacket—your DGB maintains consistent position and accessibility to your defensive handgun on top of the outermost layer of your clothing.

You can choose a DGB that will fit any occasion, from formal to casual!

One example is two women who dress in the same style – jeans with a belt and cowboy boots. One prefers to carry a waistband holster on her belt or other locations on her body. The other prefers to carry her handgun in a DGB, which allows her to go from jeans during the work week to a dress on Sunday, knowing that she always has access to her handgun regardless of attire.

A Daily Go Bag supports freedom of movement at home or work. You've secured your DGB within your control while keeping it readily accessible. This allows you to perform chores, play with the kids on the floor, or do whatever activities you need to do daily without exposing a handgun in your waistband holster or having it poke you in the ribs.

Access to your handgun is easier from a DGB when wearing outerwear in harsh conditions

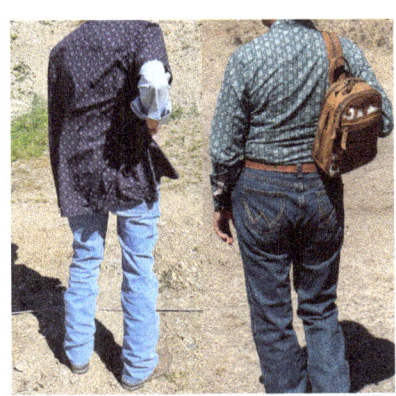

Same style dress with different modes of concealed carry

Physical, medical, and mobility challenges (e.g. wheelchairs) can leave a person vulnerable to threats from violent people and prevent traditional methods of carry. These challenges may also reduce someone's ability to avoid or respond to violence. Using a DGB provides a possible solution and the capability to defend themselves.

Women who have carried traditionally detest using the restroom. A DGB solves this problem as the bag stays on your body!

A retired LE officer, when he heard about the topic of this book, admitted that he carried "off-body" at work! His agency frowned upon plain clothes officers wearing their guns in the office. So whenever he had to attend a meeting there, he put his trusty Colt 1911 in a briefcase. Although teased about the briefcase at meetings, no one ever asked what he had in it!

Chapter 2

Deciding to Carry a Handgun

Why do you carry a handgun? Have you decided you could shoot someone who was a threat to your life?

Claim your own magnificence. Are you important enough to protect?

> You may have to use your handgun to protect yourself, and that may involve injury or death to yourself or someone else. If you cannot handle your handgun with skill when you need to use it to defend yourself, you may be seriously injured or even killed.
>
> *Vicki Farnam & Diane Nicohols from their book*
> *Women Learning to Shoot: A Guide for Law Enforcement Officers*

We recommend you follow all state and local concealed carry laws when carrying a handgun in your Daily Go Bag.

Chapter 3

Standards for the FlexCCarry℠ Daily Go Bag

FlexCCarry℠ Standards for functional carry bags (Daily Go Bag, or DGB) provide flexibility for holstering and concealing your handgun in a design of your choice. FlexCCarry℠ standards have been developed based on years of experience in daily carry, instruction in carrying a handgun in a bag, and many conversations with real-life users. These standards are meant to help you choose a handbag, sling bag, waist bag, tote bag, backpack, or briefcase, for example. Be flexible!

Standards: Dedicated Pocket

Daily Go Bags must have a dedicated pocket for the concealed holster.

- No matter how many individual pockets a bag has, one pocket must be dedicated to a holster to hold the handgun for concealed carry purposes. This dedicated pocket for the holster reduces clutter from other items that would impede a clean and efficient draw.

- The inside of the dedicated pocket should have high-strength VELCRO™ on the side which will be against the operator's body.

- The holster, secured inside the dedicated pocket with VELCRO™, must cover the trigger and hold the handgun securely in the dedicated pocket.

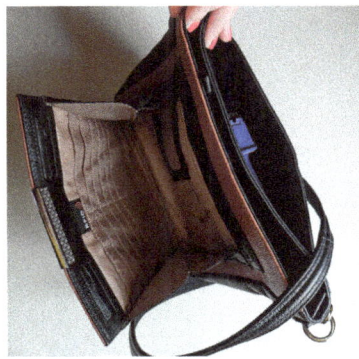

A single dedicated pocket for the handgun, separate from the pocket for personal items

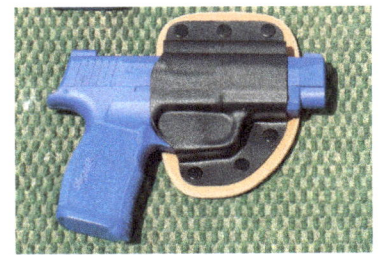

Holster must cover the trigger guard

Top entry, left/right entry, and three-sided entry dedicated pockets

- Acceptable access options to the dedicated pocket include top entry, left or right entry (to suit the operator's carry side), or three-sided entry.

- When possible, the interior lining of the dedicated pocket should enhance visibility by being light or high-visibility color (not black).

High visibility interior color and room for a magazine carrier

- The dedicated pocket may also contain a magazine carrier if there is room.

Standards: Material Performance and Type

Material Performance

The body of the Daily Go Bag should do the following:

- Support the weight of a handgun and any optional gear such as extra magazines, flashlight, OC spray, knife, or first aid items.

- Retain its shape and protect the contents while comfortably supporting the weight of the contents without sagging.

- Prevent detection or "printing" of the shape of the handgun through the fabric or leather.

- Be durable enough to withstand long-term use.

- Endure heat and sun without becoming overly soft or losing shape and sagging.

- Protect from and survive in inclement weather such as rain or snow.

Adjustable shoulder strap

- Have adjustable straps long enough to sling over a shoulder or across the body.

Material Type

Recommended materials:

- Leather of sturdy quality, either stiff or supple (depending upon personal taste)

- Woven nylon (such as Denier rating above 300D or Kevlar).

- Stout canvas

- Waxed cotton

The author received a concealed carry bag as a gift nearly 40 years ago. The bag has a combined VELCRO™/snap closure on the dedicated pocket and includes a leather holster snapped into the dedicated pocket. She carried this bag with a snubnosed revolver for many years. The sturdy quality of this bag is incredible. It locks nearly the same as it did when she received the bag. **We think you'll agree!**

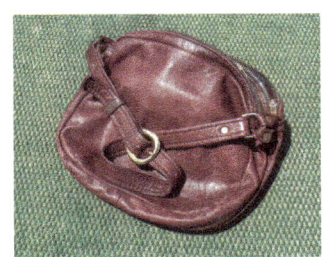

The author's first FlexCCarry℠ DGB

Standards: Hardware

Daily Go Bag hardware should meet the following specifications:

- Zipper performance is critical for a clean and efficient draw. Zippers should be self-healing or luxury-grade and hand-polished for smooth opening and closing.

- Zipper pulls should be sturdy and easy to use. Key locks or clasp locks are optional.

Specialty zipper pulls include clasped, oversized, and key lock variations

- Swivels should be sturdy enough to handle the weight of the bag contents on the straps.

- Buckles should be adjustable.

- D-rings and O-rings should be heavy-duty (which will not split apart).

Various examples of sturdy hardware for strap attachments

- Magnets, snaps and VELCRO™ must be strong enough to stay closed even when the Daily Go Bag is turned upside down, and contents fall against the magnet or snap.

- All hardware must be functional as designed.

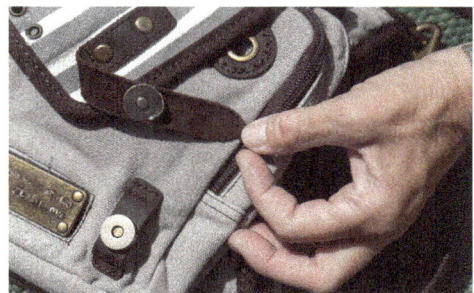

Strong magnetic snaps

Buying a good, quality Daily Go Bag costs some money, and, if buying from a reputable manufacturer, you will grow tired of the bag before it wears out. Daily Go Bags that meet all FlexCCarry℠ standards start around $75 and can range up to $400. **Spend the money; your life is worth it!**

Chapter 4

FlexCCarry℠ Daily Go Bag Options

Choose a FlexCCarry℠ Daily Go Bag that fits your lifestyle. There are many Daily Go Bag styles and options available:

Traditional handbags

Backpacks

Messenger bag, tote bag, and a waistpack

Chest rig

Thigh rig

There are also concealed carry options that you can have on your desk or your lap during a meeting, such as a planner, padfolio, or tablet case. Other options include magnetic holsters that can be attached to your car or even holsters that can be attached to your saddle. There is something to fit everyone's needs!

Options are available as briefcases, planners, folios, and tablet cases

Chapter 5

Holsters for your FlexCCarry℠ Daily Go Bag

A holster serves several purposes: 1) to hold and secure a handgun in the dedicated pocket, 2) to cover the trigger guard, and 3) to ensure consistent acquisition of your master grip.

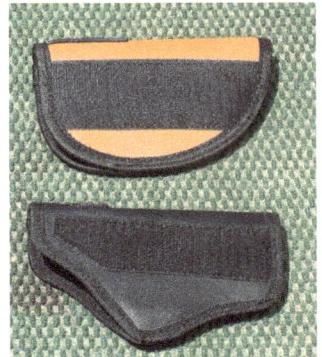
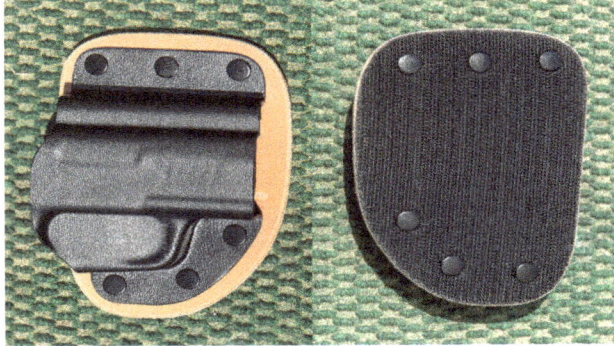

Generic nylon holsters   **VELCRO™ backed Kydex handgun-specific holster**

Holsters may be made from various materials, from nylon, which provides marginal structure, to molded leather or plastic (e.g., Kydex). The structure of the holster is significant because it prevents the holster from collapsing, which will hinder the smooth re-holstering of your handgun, and it ensures the trigger guard is covered.

Holsters with effective fit

The Daily Go Bag you purchased may not have come with a holster, or the holster provided may not fulfill these required functions. When that is the case, take it upon yourself to acquire a handgun-specific holster that can be velcroed in place to ensure a consistent master grip and that the trigger guard is covered.

An appropriate fit is dependent upon the combination of the handgun and the

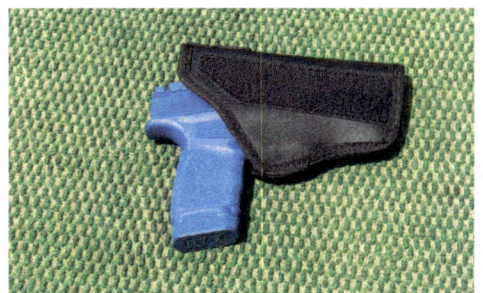 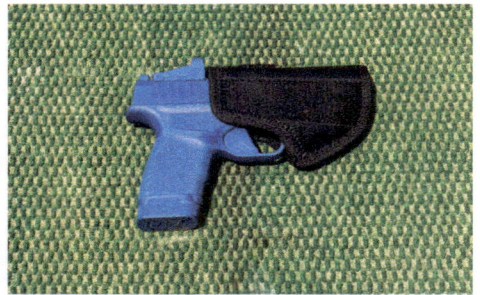

Mismatched holsters and handguns that do not fit (too big and too little)

holster fitting into the space of the dedicated pocket of your Daily Go Bag.

When your handgun has either an optic, flashlight, laser, or extended magazines, there are additional considerations to ensure that the holster fits the handgun, secures the handgun in place, covers the trigger, ensures consistent access to your master grip, and allows the dedicated pocket to close securely. **Find the right manufactured holster. Don't alter your holster to make it fit your handgun.**

The attached optic keeps this handgun from fitting entirely in this holster

Reminder: *Re-holstering is one of the most dangerous things we do with handguns.*

Chapter 6

FlexCCarry℠ Daily Go Bag Methods

The FlexCCarry℠ Daily Go Bag methods are the fundamentals of effective off-body concealed carry skills and knowledge for personal protection. The FlexCCarry℠ Methods incorporate the well-known four safety rules, as well as additional safety considerations to remember as you set up and use your Daily Go Bag.

Safety

You need to be aware of the four safety rules. If you're not familiar with the safety rules, please find them, read them, and live them.

Four Safety Rules as applied to handguns in the Daily Go Bag:

1. Treat all handguns as though they are loaded.
2. Be sure the muzzle is pointed in a safe direction.
3. Your finger goes to the trigger ONLY when the handgun is at eye level, the sights are aligned with your target, and you have made the decision to fire.
4. Be sure of your target and what is beyond it.

See Them. Read Them. Learn Them. Live Them.

Consistency in both handgun and Daily Go Bag handling is mandatory. You have a huge burden of responsibility when making the decision to carry a concealed handgun. Safety must come to mind every time 1) you pick up the DGB, 2) take off the DGB and put it down and 3) any circumstance where your hand goes to the master grip on the handgun.

There is such a variety of DGB options that when drawing and re-holstering, you need to be diligent about keeping your finger on the frame of the handgun and off the trigger, with the muzzle pointed in a safe direction.

You must know the make, model and caliber of your handgun and how it functions. That includes being sure that you don't inadvertently bump any controls on the handgun (e.g., the trigger, the magazine release button, manual safety) during the draw or re-holstering. If you bump any controls, the gun may have an accidental or negligent discharge, or it may not feed a new round when you intentionally decide to fire the handgun. Both of these situations are critical safety issues.

Setting up Your FlexCCarry℠ Daily Go Bag

Once you have made your choice from the multitude of Daily Go Bags that meet the FlexCCarry℠ standards, you need to set up your DGB for everyday use.

DGB with adjustable straps

DGB with non-adjustable straps

- **Adjust the strap** to the length that you want and need to provide accessibility to the dedicated pocket. If the strap is non-adjustable, only you can determine if the bag is usable for your body mechanics.

- **Assess the way you open and close** the dedicated pocket (zipper, magnets, size of the pull tabs). You may want to add a larger pull tab to open the dedicated pocket more easily, as well as decide where to stage the pull tab for efficient access.

DGB with large zipper pull tab

- **Orient the holster** in the dedicated pocket so that the holster (without the handgun) fits in the pocket.

- **Insert an empty magazine in the magazine well** of an empty handgun and insert the handgun into the holster. NOTE: The magazine changes the dimensions of the handgun and the way it fits into the dedicated pocket. It

Holster empty and with handgun

is important to have an empty magazine inserted in order to have the correct dimensions. Place the holster with the handgun inside the dedicated pocket. Adjust the position of the holster as needed to ensure that you can acquire a master grip when the handgun is seated in the holster.

- **Assess and confirm your hand will fit into the dedicated pocket** with enough space to acquire the master grip and draw the handgun smoothly. Hands come in many different sizes. Adjust the position of the holster until your hand moves easily to acquire the master grip.

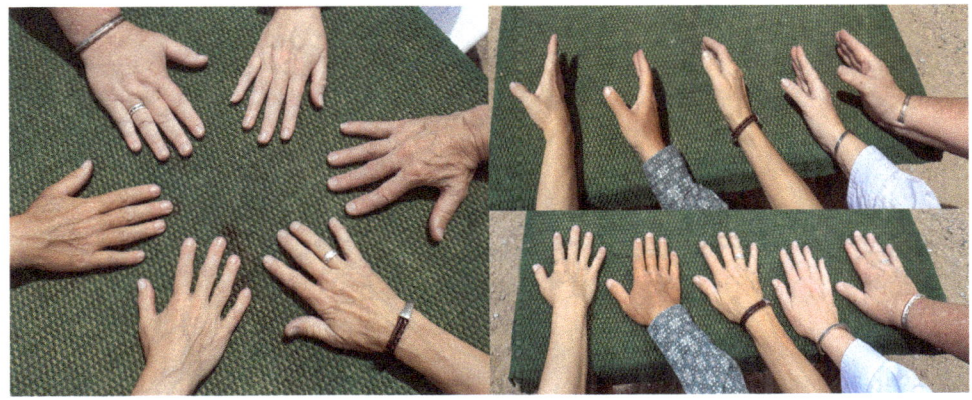

Your hand is unique - find a solution that works for your own needs

- **Lastly, close the dedicated pocket.** If the pocket doesn't close, adjust the holster until it does. If adjustments don't work, select a different combination of bag, holster, and handgun that does.

None of these combinations are effective for the gun, hand, or holster sizes

What you have just done is set up the dedicated pocket for use!

The steps of the draw are explained in the next chapter. To practice the draw, we recommend that you purchase a "blue gun" in the make and model of your real handgun. There is often a slight difference (different weights and different overall sizes with extended magazines or optics) between the blue gun and your real handgun. When you start practicing, you may be surprised by the weight of a fully loaded handgun and extra magazine!

Once you are ready to practice with a loaded handgun, practice only on a live-fire range.

Additional considerations in setting up your Daily Go Bag:

- **Wear cross body bags with the pocket on the outside of your strong side.** This way, you can draw directly to the threat. Wearing the bag on your support side would require a "cross draw." We do not recommend a cross draw because it is far too easy to muzzle your own hand, arm or an innocent bystander.

- **The weight of the handgun in the Daily Go Bag should be balanced** so as not to create physical issues.

Dedicated pocket on the outside of the strong side

- **Daily Go Bags that have a left or right-side draw may need to be pulled forward to the front of the body** while applying downward pressure to access the dedicated pocket easily.

Pulling the bag foward with pressure creates stability

- **Daily Go Bags that have the dedicated pocket on the back of the bag may need to be reversed** so that the dedicated pocket is facing outward to allow easier access to acquire the master grip.

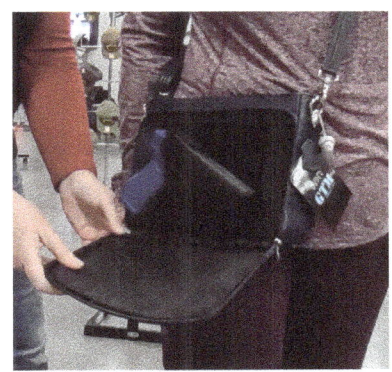

Dedicated pocket worn outside while the decorative side faces the body

- **Consider keeping the contents of your bag** to self-defense (gun, extra magazine, OC spray, flashlight, and possibly a knife) and personal essentials only. This may include re-thinking what is included in your "essentials."

21

Chapter 7

Steps of the Draw from the FlexCCarry℠ Daily Go Bag

Learning to draw and re-holster from the FlexCCarry℠ Daily Go Bag dedicated pocket is a critical component for your training for readiness. "Blue guns" are a realistic and safe alternative to live firearms while training. When learning this process, it is essential to practice first with a blue gun, then with an empty handgun with an empty magazine in the magazine well, and finally with a loaded handgun. Once you are ready to practice with a loaded handgun, practice only on a live fire range.

Here is a "blue gun" (right) with the handgun it models (left)

Wearing Your DGB on Your Strong Side

The "strong side" refers to the dominant side of the body, usually the side where you are naturally stronger and more coordinated. Most people use this side to hold and operate their firearm, typically with their dominant hand. Wear your DGB so that the opening to the dedicated pocket is easily reached from your strong side and the draw is not impeded by the strap.

Every bag is different. Make accommodations as needed to ensure that your strong arm and hand have a free and clear path to the dedicated pocket to acquire the master grip.

See the photos in this chapter for examples in different bag styles.

The FlexCCarry℠ Draw – Overview

There are seven steps to draw a handgun from your FlexCCarry℠ Daily Go Bag. Regardless which bag is used, these seven steps remain the same.

1. **Stablize the DGB:** Stabilize the FlexCCarry℠Daily Go Bag by hooking the thumb of your support hand under the strap and running it down to the point where the strap connects with the bag. For a waistbag, grab the belt strap where it attaches to the bag. Apply downward pressure to create tension for stability. Continue this downward pressure and tension until the handgun has cleared the dedicated pocket, and the handgun has moved past the support hand.

2. **Open the dedicated pocket:** Open the dedicated pocket with your strong hand. Use the zipper pull tab, or insert your thumb to push/pull the zipper open, or use your fingers to separate the magnets/VELCRO™, or lift a flap.

3. **Acquire the master grip:** Acquire a solid master grip with the strong hand high on the handgun's grip. Keep the trigger finger outside of the holster, and then on the frame when the handgun is withdrawn. **At no time should the muzzle point at the support hand, nor in any other unsafe direction.**

4. **Lift and clear:** Lift the handgun from the holster and clear it from the dedicated pocket. **At no time should the muzzle point at the support hand, nor in any other unsafe direction.**

5. **Rock and lock:** Rotate the handgun until the muzzle is parallel to the ground, if necessary, and pointed down range toward the target. **At no time should the muzzle point at the support hand, nor in any other unsafe direction.**

6. **Join hands and extend:** Move the handgun forward, past the support hand, and join hands together without pointing the handgun at the support hand.

7. **Align sights on the target:** Bring the handgun to eye level, aimed in at the target. Finger stays off the trigger until the sights are aligned on the target and the decision to fire has been made.

The FlexCCarry℠ Steps to Re-holster - Overview

There are four steps to return a handgun to the holster in your FlexCCarry℠ Daily Go Bag. Regardless which bag is used, these four steps remain the same.

1. **Stabilize the DGB:** Stabilize the FlexCCarry℠Daily Go Bag by hooking the thumb of your support hand under the strap. Run your thumb down to the point where the strap connects with the bag, applying downward pressure to create tension. Maintain this downward pressure.

2. **Bring back to pocket:** Bring the handgun back to the dedicated pocket, making sure the muzzle is pointed either still in a downrange direction or straight down at the ground, never pointing the muzzle at your support hand. Be sure your trigger finger is on the frame and off the trigger.

3. **Insert directly back into the holster:** When the handgun is directly aligned with the holster in the dedicated pocket, change the angle of the handgun as needed so that it can then be inserted smoothly back into the holster. Keep your finger in register (off the trigger, on the frame) and muzzle away from your support hand while maintaining your master grip. Make sure your thumb is on the back of the slide to prevent the slide from being pushed backward out of battery.

4. **Close the dedicated pocket.** Fasten the zipper, magnets, or VELCRO™closure for the dedicated pocket.

Side Draw with Magnet Closure: Steps to Draw

Here's what the draw looks like for a right-handed operator with a side draw dedicated pocket with a magnet closure.

1. Stabilize the DGB

2. Open the dedicated pocket

3. Acquire the master grip

4. Lift and clear

5. Rock and lock

6. Join hands and extend

7. Align sights on the target

Side Draw with Magnet Closure: Steps to Re-holster

Here's what the steps to re-holster look like for a right-handed operator with a side draw dedicated pocket with a magnet closure.

1. Stabilize the DGB

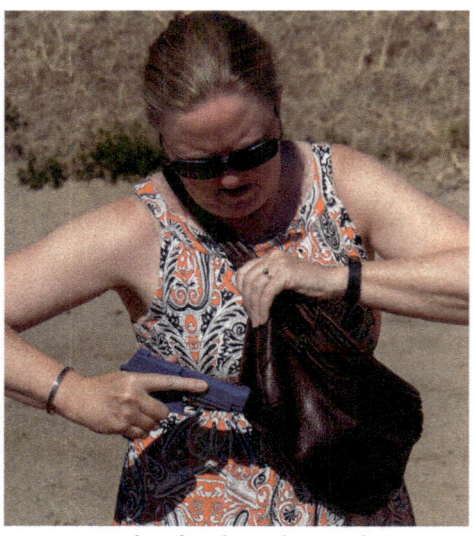

2. Bring back to the pocket

3. Insert back into the holster

4. Close the pocket

NOTES

Top Entry: Steps to Draw

Here's what the draw looks like for a left-handed operator with a top draw dedicated pocket with a zipper closure.

1. Stabilize the DGB

2. Open the dedicated pocket

3. Acquire the master grip

4. Lift and clear

5. Rock and lock

6. Join hands and extend

7. Align sights on the target

Top Entry: Steps to Re-holster

Here's what the re-holster steps look like for a left-handed operator with a top draw dedicated pocket with a zipper closure.

1. Stabilize the DGB

2. Bring back to pocket

3 Insert back into the holster

4. Close the pocket

NOTES:

Top Draw with Flap and Zipper Closure: Steps to Draw

Here's what the draw looks like for a right-handed operator with a top draw dedicated pocket with a flap and zipper closure.

1. Stabilize the DGB

2. Open the dedicated pocket

3. Acquire the master grip

4. Lift and clear

5. Rock and lock

6. Join hands and extend

7. Align sights on the target

Top Draw with Flap and Zipper Closure: Steps to Re-holster

Here's what the steps to reholster look like for a right-handed operator with a top draw dedicated pocket with a flap and zipper closure.

1.a Stabilize the DGB

1.b Lift flap

2. Bring back to pocket

3. Insert back into the holster

**4.a Close the pocket:
Fasten the zipper**

**4.b Close the pocket:
Secure the flap**

NOTES:

Sling Strap Backpack: Steps to Draw

Here's what the draw looks like for a right-handed operator with a sling strap backpack.

1.a Thumb on strap

1.b Bring bag to chest

1.c Stabilize the DGB

2. Open the dedicated pocket

3. Acquire the master grip

4. Lift and clear

5. Rock and lock

6. Join hands and extend

7. Align sights on the target

Sling Strap Backpack: Steps to Re-holster

Here's what the steps to re-holster looks like for a right-handed operator with a sling strap backpack.

1. Stabilize the DGB

2. Bring back to pocket

3. Insert back into the holster

4. Close the pocket

NOTES:

Single Strap Backpack: Steps to Draw

Here's what the draw looks like for a left-handed operator with a single strap backpack.

1.a Thumb on strap

1.b Bring bag to chest

1.c Stabilize the DGB

2. Open the dedicated pocket

3. Acquire the master grip

NOTE: This is a cross draw, requiring extensive practice to ensure that the muzzle stays pointed down until lifted and cleared for rotate, rock and lock.

4. Lift and clear

5. Rotate, rock and lock

6. Join hands and extend

7. Align sights on the target

Single Strap Backpack: Steps to Re-holster

Here's what the steps to re-holster look like for a left-handed operator with a single strap backpack.

NOTE: Re-holstering across the body requires extensive practice to ensure that the muzzle stays pointed down so that you don't muzzle yourself or anyone else.

1. Stabilize the DGB

2. Rotate and align with the holster

3. Insert back into the holster

4. Close the pocket

IMPORTANT: While it is difficult to discern in these photos, the muzzle is never pointed at the body nor arm. It is actually pointing at the void between them.

NOTES:

Side Draw with Vertical Zipper Closure: Steps to Draw

Here's what the draw looks like for a right-handed operator with a side draw dedicated pocket with a vertical zipper closure.

1. Stabilize the DGB

2. Open the dedicated pocket

3. Acquire the master grip

4. Lift and clear

5. Rock and lock

6. Join hands and extend

7. Align sights on the target

Side Draw with Vertical Zipper Closure: Steps to Re-holster

Here's what the steps to re-holster look like for a right-handed operator with a side draw dedicated pocket with a vertical zipper closure.

1. Stabilize the DGB

2. Bring back to pocket

3. Insert back into the holster

4. Close the pocket

NOTES:

Side Draw with Vertical Zipper Closure: Steps to Draw

Here's what the draw looks like for a left-handed operator with a side draw dedicated pocket with a vertical zipper closure.

1. Stabilize the DGB

2. Open the dedicated pocket

3. Acquire the master grip

4. Lift and clear

5. Rock and lock

6. Join hands and extend

7. Align sights on the target

Side Draw with Vertical Zipper Closure: Steps to Re-holster

Here's what the steps to re-holster look like for a left-handed operator with a side draw dedicated pocket with a vertical zipper closure.

1. Stabilize the DGB

2. Bring back to pocket

3. Insert back into the holster

4. Close the pocket

Practice! Practice! Practice!

Blue gun, unloaded handgun, loaded handgun on a live fire range.

Consistency is the goal!

NOTES:

Chapter 8

The FlexCCarry℠ Daily Go Bag as a Storage Container

There are two functions of any FlexCCarry℠ Daily Go Bag. One is as a method of concealment, such as carrying your handgun with you on your body. Secondly, when it is removed from your body and left unattended, any Daily Go Bag becomes a "storage container." The positive point is that the Daily Go Bag conceals your handgun so that no one knows it is inside the Daily Go Bag when you take it off your body and set it down, unlike removing your handgun and holster from your belt where it would be visible to anyone.

DGB and holstered handgun removed from the belt

Other typical bags and storage containers

You are responsible for making sure your Daily Go Bag does not fall into irresponsible hands. The fact that the handgun is not visible doesn't matter. If some unauthorized person picks up your Daily Go Bag, takes it away, or opens it and removes the handgun, there is always the potential for danger and injury to anyone.

The Daily Go Bag is no different than a range bag, gun bag, gun case, rifle case, gun rug, duty belt, typical go bag, or original gun box that gun owners have in their home, car, office, range, hunting camp or anywhere else they store their guns. Even a secured lockbox next to your night table can be picked up and stolen. All of those devices require conscientious decisions for appropriate storage. **You are responsible!**

Some FlexCCarry℠ Daily Go Bags have dedicated pockets that can be locked with a key or secured with a clip. Do you lock or secure the dedicated pocket? It's your choice to determine what works for you in your circumstances. Recognize that locking/securing the dedicated pocket will cause some delay when you access the pocket. If you lock the dedicated pocket when you set the Daily Go Bag down, you must build unlocking it into your routine when you pick it up.

Various Key Locks and Interlock Zipper Pulls

How do you balance safety and readiness for self-defense? The more safely secured your handgun is, the less ready it is. The more ready it is, the less it is safely secured. Even if you use the solution of a safe that is too heavy to move, a vault bolted into your vehicle, or a cable locking device, we still have the trade-off of safety versus readiness for self-defense.

Chapter 9

Using Your FlexCCarry℠ Daily Go Bag

The purpose of using your Daily Go Bag is to have an effective means to defend your life. FlexCCarry℠ solutions, methods, and training offer many ways to make that happen. Choices can range from avoidance, de-escalation, disengagement, or defensive action.

Your FlexCCarry℠ Daily Go Bag allows you to respond instantly and offers a surprise to your assailant. Your DGB can be set up to carry not only a handgun, extra magazine, or knife but also less lethal options like a conducted electrical weapon (such as a stun gun), OC spray, or flashlight. It is also a good idea to include a separate waistband holster in your DGB to manage unknown circumstances. Your DGB becomes an immediate response kit when you include a tourniquet and other first aid essentials such as an IBD (Israeli Battle Dressing).

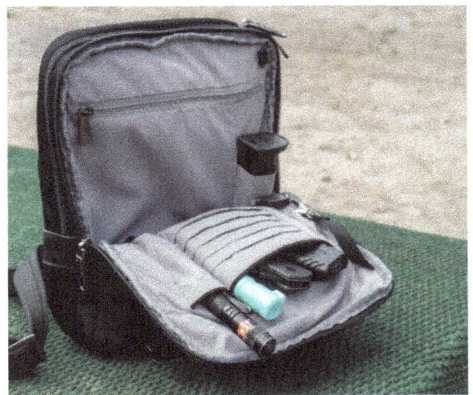

Less lethal options

IBD and tourniquet

> The surprise element of carrying a handgun in your Daily Go Bag saved a woman in the parking lot of a big box store. She attracted attention because she is an attractive woman, well dressed, wearing a Rolex and an Apple Watch, and was headed to her Mercedes car, which was parked away from other vehicles. As she approached her car, two men stepped between her and her vehicle and asked if she needed assistance putting items in her car. Her immediate response was to reach into her Daily Go Bag, which she was carrying. She had her master grip on her handgun, but it was not visible. The men must have suspected she was carrying a handgun because they quickly changed their minds, told her to have a good day, and left her alone, allowing her to continue safely to her vehicle.

FlexCCarry℠ Daily Go Bag Standards apply to both women and men because the variety of bags offer solid solutions and appealing choices that are not based on gender.

The ultimate goal is to be prepared to respond to a threat on demand. Be sure your handgun is loaded!

Chapter 10

Training to Use Your FlexCCarry℠ Daily Go Bag

The ultimate goal is to be prepared to respond to a threat on demand. Training is the way to acquire the knowledge, skills, and competence you need to save your life.

Seek training in areas that will enhance your self-defense skills and knowledge, such as the fundamentals of handgun handling, tactics, movement, accuracy, and avoidance. Scenario-based training, simulators, and role-playing exercises are excellent ways to test your decision-making skills and to fail without severe consequences. Women, in particular, don't like to fail! However, we can seek growth-mindset-based training where failure pushes us to correct instead of leaving us stuck in the same spot.

Seek out training that is relevant to you and your life. If you are a person with disabilities, find an instructor who can understand your disability and help you be successful with your DGB. Don't be discouraged; there are many non-traditional ways to learn self-defense skills.

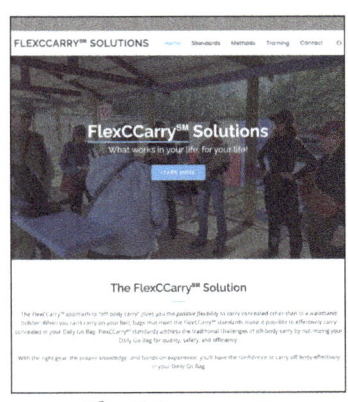

The FlexCCarry℠ Solution

FlexCCarry.com

Training does not stop at the end of a class. Review and analyze your training to identify what works for you in your everyday life or what works for you in that moment of extreme anxiety. Use your Daily Go Bag in your training and your everyday life. Make it part of the way you will resolve a threat.

FlexCCarry℠ Certified Instructors are available across the country. Refer to the www.FlexCCarry.com website to identify an instructor near you and seek training.

If you love what you have read in this guide and are interested in becoming a FlexCCarry℠ Certified Instructor or hosting an Instructor class, refer to the course description and schedule found at the www.Defense-Training.com website.

Additional information on the author and other classes she offers can be found on the www.DTIwomen.com website. Or, contact vicki@flexccarry.com to learn more or share your personal experiences with off-body carry.

Chapter 11

Closing Comments

Everyone who makes the decision to go armed *"for* their life" must address the myriad challenges of doing so *"in* their life."

As the factors in each of our lives make us individuals, we must consider those factors when deciding which FlexCCarry℠ solution will best suit our own specific needs.

Regardless, the decisions should be made from a sound foundation of knowledge and understanding unique to each armed citizen.

The chapters found in this book will provide you with that foundation. Experience dictates that training and practice will make that foundation firm.

We encourage you to claim your own magnificence. Use your agile and flexible mind to seek the answers to your questions and find the method of carry that works best for you.

Glossary

Accuracy – Hitting the target where you intend to hit.

Battery - The slide is completely forward.

Blue gun – An inert detailed replica of specific handgun brands and models.

Finger in register – Your finger is placed flat along the frame above the trigger and trigger guard of your handgun. There are two places for your trigger finger when you are holding your handgun: in the register position when you are not shooting or on the trigger when your sights are on the target, and you have made the decision to shoot.

Finger on the trigger – The position of your finger when the sights are on target, and the decision to fire has been made.

Gun fit – The size of a handgun in relation to the size of your hand determines how well the handgun fits. A handgun that fits allows you to acquire a proper grip and trigger finger placement easily.

Loaded gun – If a handgun has a round of ammunition in the chamber, it is considered loaded.

Magazine – A metal or polymer container inserted into the magazine well of an autoloading handgun that holds the rounds of ammunition in position until they are loaded into the chamber.

Master grip – The strong hand is as high as possible on the gun grip under the tang, the trigger finger is high on the frame above the trigger (register position), and the remaining fingers are wrapped around the grip.

Muzzle – The end of the barrel where the bullet exits.

Muzzle awareness – Knowing where the muzzle is pointed when the handgun is in your hand.

Register position – (See above - *Finger in register*)

Safe direction – A backstop that will contain, absorb, or stop bullets.

Trigger finger – The index finger of your strong hand. If you switch your handgun to a master grip in your support hand, the index finger of your support hand will be your trigger finger.

Unloaded gun – A handgun that does not have a round of ammunition in the chamber.

Resource List

Recommended Reading

Teaching Women to Shoot: A Law Enforcement Instructor's Guide
by Vicki Farnam and Diane Nicholl

Women Learning to Shoot: A Guide for Law Enforcement Officers
by Diane Nicholl and Vicki Farnam

The Farnam Method of Defensive Handgunning, Second Edition
by John S. Farnam

All three of the books listed above and more are available through:
https://defense-training.com

Gun Tote'n Mamas® Purse Owner's Manual
https://bit.ly/GTMPurseOwnersManual

The Cornered Cat: A Woman's Guide to Concealed Carry
by Kathy Jackson - https://www.corneredcat.com

The Law of Self Defense
by Andrew Branca - https://lawofselfdefense.com

The Gift of Fear
by Gavin DeBecker - https://gdba.com

Deep Survival
by Laurence Gonzales - http://www.laurencegonzales.com

Surviving Survival
by Laurence Gonzales - http://www.laurencegonzales.com

Deadly Force: Understanding Your Right to Self Defense
by Massad Ayoob - https://massadayoobgrcup.com

On Killing
by Lt. Col. Dave Grossman - https://grossmanontruth.com

Reputable Manufacturers

The following manufacturers are known to create quality bags, holsters, and other concealed-carry gear. Some of their products appear in the examples shown in this book. We recommend starting here when looking for your FlexCCarry℠ bag and holster. That said, it is important to check the attributes of each product for yourself to determine if they meet FlexCCarry℠ standards and if they are an appropriate fit for your specific and unique needs.

This listing is for your benefit as a starting point—it is not an official endorsement for any specific product.

* GTM Originals . . . . .www.gtmoriginals.com

* Ukoala Carry Bags by Mayan . . .www.uubgear.com

* Zendira. . . . . .www.zendira.com

* Travelon . . . . .www.travelonbags.com

* UC Leather. . . . . .www.ucleathercompany.com

* Vertx. . . . . .www.vertx.com

* First Tactical . . . . .www.firsttactical.com

* Galco Gun Leather. . . . . .www.galcogunleather.com

* Crossbreed Holsters . . . . .www.crossbreedholsters.com

* Ring's Manufacturing . . . . .www.blueguns.com

* 5.11 Tactical www.511tactical.com

* Cameleon Bags . . . . .www.cameleonbags.com

* Coronado Leather . . . . .www.coronadoleather.com

We are always interested in learning about new companies with quality products that meet FlexCCarry℠ standards. If you have a recommendation for a company to add to this list, please contact us by email at info@flexccarry.com.

NOTES: